Soul Pilgrim

Soul Pilgrim

Robert Howe

ᚠ

Ab Æterno Press

First published in 2024
by Ab Aeterno Press
9 Grove Place
Minehead, Somerset
TA24 6EN

Typeset in 11/14 pt serif
Printed and bound in Great Britain by Amazon.com, Inc

A CIP catalogue record of this book is available from the
British LIbrary.

ISBN 978-1-3999-4808-1

For Ayla

Contents

Contents

Contents

"But perhaps we may make our stand along the *edge* of that civilization, like a magician, or like a person who, having lived among another tribe, can no longer wholly return to his own. He lingers half within and half outside of his community, open as well, then, to the shifting voices and flapping forms that crawl and hover beyond the mirrored walls of the city."

DAVID ABRAM
The Spell of the Sensuous

Prologue

LAMENT, MY BELOVED

dreamless nights
filled with silent screams

I'm lost in my life

and I'm trying to find
some meaning

I'm lost in my life

and I can't help
screaming

out for help
behind dead eyes
partying into
headlights of oblivion

dead like the rabbit
trapped
I'm all out of fucks
my soul is being sucked

please
        come
                save me

falling past the point
of no return

these are perilous times
to be alive in

caught in a lie
deep down disbelieving
that the good life is the job
model wife   decent whip
drinking craft beer and
all the other jazz that
makes the whipped
                              of which

on top is the cherry

ego making merry
at its success of conquest
and domination   when inside
all is a mess   hesitation
deep grief and pain
at the realisation
the one chance I have
is being wasted on
the house of cards

made from lies so best resort
to lines   pills   sex
and other cheap thrills
to feed charybdis who's hunger
can   never   be   sated

with such empty vices

lament

I'm lost in my life
and I'm trying to find
some meaning

I'm lost in my life
and I can't help
screaming
out for help
behind dead eyes

partying into
headlights of
oblivion

> I've fallen past
> the point of no return

dreamless nights
filled with silent screams

I'm doing what I can
to live a life of truth

going through my days
empty and confused

> I've fallen past
> the point of no return

at the threshold
the fire burns

Communion

FOR LIFE

The colour of bark,
   the green needles,
     the brown ferns,
       the blue sky beyond.

The silver sun,
   long shadows,
     squirrels playing,
       the forest standing as one.

The beauty, the severity,
   the stillness and movement.

This, my friends,
   is what its all for.

WITHIN REACH

Everything is alive,
   can you feel it?

Palpable and rich
   within grasp and touch,

like a rainbow - you
   know its there

right before you
   and all around,

but if you grasp it
   you'll find empty space.

Now, see the grace
   of the floating clouds

or the splendour
   of a sun rise

and wherever you look
   find it - there inside,

where does it live
   within you?

EVERGREEN

Standing tall and proud these
evergreens sway,

fir and spruce
and others with many names.

peering through the earth,
they're met by swaying heads
and creaking trunks,

amongst them
I muse life,
slowing the racing mind.

I remember a distant memory -

that the trees and birds,
the late blooming gorse
are all here to greet me,

they all long to meet me

and drown me
in their sea of whispers.

AN INTELLIGENCE

There was an intelligence
that took the form of a seed
and grew into a tree - a tall pine.

Every moment was a choice,

How tall do I grow?
How hard does my wood need to be?
The leaves I need are...
long and thin.

This intelligence, its form,
is defined by its shape,
by its unique way of being in the world.

That is the form of pine,
fir, larch,

the world we know.

SECOND HOME

The silty waters
kicked by the currents
shield my way from me.

What to do
in such an instance?

Return, of course,
to my second home,
that place
no other human knows,

in which
I can shed

and resign
all the names
and roles
that tie me
to my life
and keep me small.

THE SILENCE

I   can   see   the   silence

not for very long,
but I catch a   glimpse
when I hear amblers in the distance
talking of their worldly affairs.

　A shrill of laughter
finds its way to me,
moving like a boat through
still waters.

In the wake of their passing
　the trees return to rest,
　　the birds return to song,
　　　the   waters   seem   to   settle
　　　　and resume their glorious song.

The silence is viscous now,
　a dance partner to the wind,
　　swirling
　　　and
　　　　moving

amongst   and   through
　all   things.

THE CORMORANT

on edge
like a cormorant

its body made for flight
in air and beneath waves

it nestles on jagged rocks
beyond the cliff's face

perched
          on the last stretched fingers of rock

lost to the breaking surf

          the wind a wall

the bird with its kin
                    unmoving

at home
on the naked faces

knowing
          just knowing

it will move when need ignites it
   when impulse takes it

      content to be between

rain   rock
   sea   and   wind

A MOMENT AT HIGH TIDE

The sweet green air
and salty blue breeze
mix and wash

breathing out the day,
letting the sterile and stiff
wash away,

white plumes of clouds
are kissed golden
by the parting sun,

raked pebbles
dragged by receding waves
have their voids replaced
by the next one
and so on;

a brief moment of respite
a brief moment of solitude

trying to connect
and be with the very thing
I live for.

A LOVE NOTE

to breathe
   to sleep
      to wake

and experience
   the joy
      of a new day

birdsong
   announcing
      the glory

dawnlight
   showing
      the possibility

of the unknown
   stirring
      in the dew

space
   in silence
      reaching

places
   the unseeing
      know

vows of the vanquished
    mercy of the conquerors

revealing
    how we are

at our edges
    on our knees

waiting
    to receive
        whilst being

all we know
    ourselves to be

THE DISCIPLE

To teach, she learns;
a devotee to the plants
and trees, the animals
and sky.

She breaks open
and disappears,
she sheds and finds
the next crack,
breathing in respite
only when time is given.

To her children
she appears like
an all knowing magician,
their crinkled brows
wonder where her edges lie,
suspecting her knowledge
might be boundless,

but at the altar
she bows and surrenders,
gives herself over
to the grandeur of the temple,

the everlasting breath
moving through the trees,

waves breaking on the countless seas,
the seasons holding their gifts
just beyond reach - bestowed
only when she meets
the need or test.

But her service is never known -
this agent of secrets,
acting in plain sight,
every breath, every sinew that
moves her life is

a living prayer.

So willing to be broken open,
so willing to surrender to
dark nights that want to come,
she can wait for the blue mists
that hang at dawn,
in valleys or amongst
golden stems of wheat.

So when she gives her tender words
of care and direction,
when she lives the demonstration
to her children by just being,

the disciple is alive,
ever-present to the conversation.

OUT THERE

The weather is holy
I mean, there's a difference
between outside and in

like, when it rains
or the wind
bathes us with its mood -

there's something essential
in the place we meet the world.

Beyond taste and smell,
touch, sight and hearing

together these make
something greater

which sates
a thirst of a different kind.

With it
I know relief,

with it
I feel complete,

I am overtaken
and breathe it
as a drink -

it takes me,
it holds me,
it reminds me,

'This is Life!'

I only hear its exaltation
when I close
the door behind me

and settle
on the sofa
for the night.

Then the longing
begins again,

that ache
and agitation
for reunion

with the one place
that completes me.

THE SEASONS

I want to live. And I mean more
than just serving the image at my centre,
embodying and expressing the true shape of me.
When I say I want to live, I mean
I wish to be here on Earth
so I can come into the beauty each day
and savour the sweet cocktail
of hemlock and cypress and pine;
shaken, sometimes stirred,
by each of the season's winds,
so I can know the feeling of their teeth
on my bones, or their tender,
balm-like kisses on hot summer days.

I want to be enraptured by the singing birds,
to be lifted by the great tits crooning once more
after such long absence through the colder,
darker months.

To know and revel in the gifts
of each season:

the gold of Autumn, Winter's slowness,
the re-membrance of Spring and
the fruits of Summer. Each carves
a facet of the diamond,
their faces casting rainbows.

To know the seasons is to know life.

The warmth and smell of fire. The engulfing
majesty of stars and planets overhead.
To know the lurching dread that comes
when peering into the depths of a pool,
or an ocean one cannot see the bottom of.
I want to live to know these things
and to witness, amongst the severity
of the man-made-world, the beauty and miracles
of humans unravelling - hearing the calls of soul,
responding to the finger taps
of windswept branches on windows
and daring to go into those places unknown

aware that death is the risk, and that life is at stake
to blossom into the flower that's been sleeping,
waiting for the right time, the right season,
to blossom and emerge, to give its fragrance
and colour to the symphony.

I want to live to see and know my own children – to
witness an incarnate soul
inhabiting flesh and blood,
going through the journey of forgetting
and falling, of hearing and responding
to the vernal impulse that keeps moving.
It never goes away – only we forget
how to feel it. To know it. To trust it.

Because that pulse is more than any one person -
it's bigger and greater than that.

So vast, it threatens to smite and overwhelm us.

To know that fear for myself,
to live it at each season of my life,
at each new threshold I come to -
to live the test and say, 'yes' each time,
or as often as I can,

that is why I want to live,

so my roots may grow as deep as the trunk is tall,
so that I can hold and guide, support and love
other seeds to root, so that they too can grow and
know the good fight, be witnesses and actors of life,
so that they too may become the forest
and marvel at the clouds and know
the sweet relief of thick summer rain
falling in a way that tempts the mind
to think for a fleeting moment
that the moon might just fall from the sky.

Pilgrimage

QUESTING

The waking dream
known as your life

isn't quite where your soul
wants to be.

The trees are calling,
the waves are asking

to be met and known
for all that they are.

Feel it now -
the fire in your heart,

where does it want you
to go?

BUEN CAMINO

Which way will my path unfold?
Where does my road lead me?

These are questions our heads need to know,
but our hearts... our hearts they whisper,

Trust me
Follow me into the dark

and that place it asks you to go

can be lonely
   and scary
      and bleak.

On your journey through the wasteland
you'll likely groan and weep,
limp and suffer

in all the ways
a human body can,

but the dark night never lasts.

If you know how to pray,
if you can see with open eyes

and live the prayer
through your body,

if you can converse
and drop into ceremony,

if you are able to follow
and listen to your heart,

to give voice and words
to what wishes to be spoken,

of what it really asks

then, my friend,
the world will open to you,
it will welcome you with open arms,
it will ask you to pay a price

and jump into a pool
that will likely consume you.

But if you're not willing to jump,
to risk it all,
to put your life on the line
and dare a great fall

then why walk at all?

May each of your strides and steps
be imbued with your vitality.

May every breath be the greatest
thanksgiving you ever give.

May the pilgrims before you
fill you with their dreams
as you speak 'ultreia'
and think of past kings.

Step well my friend
into this new world

and grieve
all that you leave
behind you to die.

Buen Camino.

NOTHING CHANGES

Every moment
is an open door,

just like the minute
you were born,
all is the same -

nothing changes.

Seasons roll by,
children stop crying
and start grieving

behind closed doors.

Life is imagined
and passes by
in the blink of an eye -

nothing changes.

The environment declines,
there's the house, the wife
and fine wine;

you are scared to die
because you've never known
the meaning of a well lived life -

nothing changes.

The intelligence
of a pine cone,

the way in which
flowers grow,

the clouds dancing
upon strokes of wind -

every moment
is an open door,

just like the minute
you were born,
all is the same -

nothing changes.

First footsteps
trodden in snow,

your direction
only known by
what lives.

Having heard
and felt
the unyielding
waves of life
moving through,

now is the time
to find
all you were born with.

RAINBOWS

Today I crossed a threshold -
    from standing and waiting,
        preparing and shifting,
            the day with rainbows
                marked the threshold and its lip.

It took me two days to reach;
    on my second night,
        wet and sore,
            in pain and awash with voices

I almost stopped,
    convinced it was the loving thing to do.

But I realised that
    the purpose of my journey
        had not yet been lived

that the seed at the heart of my crossing
    had not yet sprung its radicle root,
        was yet to defy gravity and grow
            upwards to blossom and fruit.

Its not enough to pray,
    one must walk and live the prayer.

I am here,
    I am open,
        calling to be shaped
            and formed.

My bag,
    which holds my life,
        is my cross,

                my wounds already inflicted.

I look west and see the path before me.
    Behind me long shadows fall across
        the way already walked.

To the north, rising from the waters,
    are the rainbows,
        harking to the heavens and earth
            that this journey has just begun.

INVOKING THE ELEMENTS

Walking the cliff tops
through the wind and rain,
a terror lodges in my chest.

I see the timeless rocks and
a weather system overhead,
hanging over land and sea.

I'm in awe of the elements,
I respect them so deeply -

their might and power,
I call it to move through me

so I may weald it
as a craftsman,

an agent of Soul and Life,

to be a vessel for the wilds
to inhabit and fill,

so they may be known
through my body and work,

so all who encounter these words
can know the power of the gods

and know that all is done
to serve Life and it's unfolding.

SILVER MAIDEN

I sit and watch
the eternal movement

the long, stretching reflections
of clouds upon a lightly rippling sea,

the infinite white that never ceases
around outcrops of rocky teeth.

Slowly, where I come from
fades and passes,

where I go is unknown,
yet I know of the hardship to come,

but it matters not,

because the low-hanging sun warms my skin
against the cool autumnal breeze,

the season and the elements
conjoin through me

so something new,
something more is born.

It dances like a shadow,
glides silently like a spectre,
this quintessence.

It moves through me like the wind,
but I only know it's presence
when I stop and listen
to the world around me.

There I sense its edges -
dancing and moving freely,
like a silver maiden
nude beneath the moon,

her head held back in rapture,
her slender lines inviting me
to consummate the love we share.

AT THE THRESHOLD

The threshold
is the point

I look back from

endowed with the treasures
encountered and won.

With these gifts
I walk into the world,

into my life,

living from and with

all that I am...

   ...now...

...the work begins,

to live faithfully
with all riches bestowed,

the form of the image lives in the practice:

> of body,
> of mind,
> of soul.

To show up
and say yes

each day
is my task,

so my being becomes
a clear channel

for Life Force
to run through,

so Brahma
may craft

the image

Vishnu himself
is dreaming.

THE ADDICT

I was in crisis
the other day,
in the clutches
of the addict
who keeps me
highly strung.

When taken
I'm unable
to make healthy choices,

I keep
driving myself
into the ground

doing the one thing
I know
goes against
my best interest.

And even though
I know,
somehow I'm convinced
the vice - its grip
is the one thing
I need to survive.

'Its for the best'
'Just for now'
'One more'

and I'm taken,
lost and awash
in the colourless realm.

I even see myself
in the act
and still
I turn away -

although, there is
a distant disquiet,
a secret understanding

that what I do
doesn't serve

and I know it
once the deed is done.

I become highly strung,
lose my landmarks,
am unable to drop
and meet the stillness...

The morning was lost,
the day was slipping
from me.

With a quickened pulse
I rushed through
the door

and drove to the place
that was calling.

Up on the moor
at Selworthy Beacon
I walked a path
new to my feet
and descended into
Allerford Woods.

I met a narrow track,
stepped along its contour
and strayed somewhere
at its centre.

I waded across a sea
of decaying leaves
arriving in a space
held by ancient oak and holly.

I wandered to their centre
and surrendered to the earth,
asking the trees to hold me.

I groaned and sang
all that the addict needed.

Each time I do something
like this -

giving voice and shape
to the wounded within me

I am startled by the pain
and suffering they express.

Their sounds disturb me,
I am one possessed
by someone, or something else

and to think,
all this lives inside
and is contained
by my unassuming frame -

no wonder the soup spoils,
no wonder the nectar sours.

I gave myself to him
as fully as I dared,
went as far as I could
although I know the enactment
wanted to be fiercer,

such is the fury that rages.

But still I tried
and gave myself
to this essential act.

I couldn't tell you
how I knew it was done,
but I stopped at some point,
emptied.

Sprawled out, spent
I couldn't tell you where I went,
perhaps in that moment
I knew oblivion.

For I was lost,
the only presence
that stayed with me
was the wind.

Its watery voice
tethered me to the land.

When I blinked
I watched the boughs and leaves.

I always knew the air was like water,
but I'd never seen it
move as currents before,

amongst wooden arms,
conducting a symphony of sparkling leaves.

I couldn't tell you how long I lay for,
I couldn't tell you what I thought
or wanted in those moments.

All I knew,
what I sensed,
was the addict's zest
had gone.

I understood then
that he comes
when I suffer -

when I cannot cope and feel overwhelmed,

when life is too sharp
and I cannot meet myself in it.

I turn away and switch off in desperation.

Now I see
how he serves me
and I am grateful

for his devotion and service
to my temple,

what an ally.

How I'm grieved
that I need him
to cope.

But he is soothed,
although I know where he lurks,

that he wants to come
and save me when I need -

but I know that I've got this,
my life in my hands,

holding the hardest choice:

to embrace and meet myself,
completely as I do.

THERE IS NO EASY WAY

My beloved invites me
to speak my feeling
not just incidents and moments
that make up my daily round.

She asks me to dive
and go

      deeper,

to plumb the depths
and retrieve the wispy threads
that imbue my actions and thoughts.

When I start -
finding thread ends,
enticing and pulling
with my forefinger and thumb,
I begin to retrieve my colour,

I begin to see
the very things that scare me
and induce shallow sleep.

Its hard to look,
to see and know
these colours of grief and woe.

I see a sad picture
and hold it as she does.

We both acknowledge
its the worry that's new.

I groan from a weight
I've rarely known before,

but I speak and name what's here.

We both look and say,

                    Holy.

Drawing out these silver threads
offers sweet relief -

there is no fix or cure,
only the journey to contend with.

There is no easy way,
only life through death.

There is no easy way,
there can be no other way either.

GIVE/RECEIVE

The plumb line hangs
   straight and swings
     from side to side
       drawing an arc
         with its weighted end.

       Slow and steady
     it shows
    nothing is still.

    If you were to ask
  I'd say, 'I'm good'

but a myriad of forces
   shape the weight's motion.

    Its never simple
      to distil life
        in brief moments
          of exchange.

       How can you ever see
     or know
    the stories playing out

   unless you give your heart
  and flesh
to the tellings?

How do I speak the edge
or the wisps that inspire
the angst or dread
lurking in the darkness,
wanting to rise up
from within?

How do we reach these ones
and speak?

By daring
to entrust our gold
into the hands of those
undeserving or unwilling
to handle such coin?

Mighty is the act
of speaking the words
that make the house shake,

holy is the act
of receiving completely
the fragile gifts
bestowed unto
our waiting selves.

THE RISK

Every time is the greatest risk.
Every time I shudder and sigh.

Never used to be that way,
but now I understand the stakes.

It used to be fun,
but now there's also a weight.

It comes because I know
there are no guarantees,

but its the
only thing to do
to take direction,

to sink further into place
and live.

BREADCRUMBS

There's so much
to face and meet,

at first
its making
ends meet,

then there's everything
that comes in between:

living with integrity,
rooting in meaning,
self-healing and wholing,

being blown open
by the largest conversation;

and this here
is the task
at hand,

beyond car repairs
or managing neighbourly relations,

tending to health,
or navigating a move

with a pregnant partner.

With it all,
through it all,

as life happens
and unfolds,
arises and confronts,

holding space
within myself,
within my life,

just to meet
and hear -

to recognise
the subtle whispers

that appear
as breadcrumbs

inviting me
along the way.

Abduction

PIERCING

running the gauntlet of life

my,
   my,
      what a ride

never quite know
   what's gonna come

could be disease,

or love,
   or loss,
      or rapture

either way
   the feeling will come

   keenly
      and pierce you
         as a blade

you might howl
   or wince,

bleed
   or scream,

laugh
   or swallow it down,

but you can be sure
   that either way
      that thing will come
         that will touch you

it will pierce you
   and run you through
      and demand you know it

and when you feel it -
   whatever 'it' may be,

then you will know...
   you will know

            what it means to live

GRIEF

its easy
to be good
or say things are fine

its easy to brush it off
or swallow things down

to feign indifference
or pass off as non descript

but its harder
to make space
for what really lives

the drizzly
ugly colours
that rage as a storm

somewhere far away
but just within reach -

to find the edges
of these pits
and be taken by them

to scream and grunt
thrash and punch
howl, lament and cry

till your frame shakes
in a way no other thing
can inspire or induce

how I fear these places

that they might break me
or smite me

lay me flat and destroy
who I am

KEENING

The keening shriek
of remembered grief,

how the lid
blows off
and drags you

down into a pit
that may never end.
The tears
may cease

but that
blossoming ache
threatens to collapse
the sides of your sorrow,

promising the end of life
as its known.

FALLING

I'm

      falling

kicking my legs above me
      like a babe in search of its nurse

         my eyes are panic stricken

      my hands grasp
the air which runs
        through my fingers

but   the   air   is   here

brushing my hair
   up past
      my cheeks
        and face

my
   body
     knows

it is

      falling

moved by an unknown
                    force

and yet I grasp

      trying to hold

          anything I can

DEMONS

To know the grief,
to name it helps.

Now I understand
what it all means -

the unbearable ache,
the waves and tremors
of volatile emotion.

Now I understand
why I'm so angry,

its a comfort to know
the rage is true,

but something
I'm coming home to,

the ache I haven't quite
cried, or howled
or screamed or punched

is the one that comes
from deep down,

the darkest place,
the deepest pit

so far away
I might not have
met it all.

This place exists
beyond time or mind,

      it is primal

a place of untame beings,
of shapes and forms
dreams have never known.

These are the ones
that want to rise
with my anguished howls,

these are the ones
bounding for freedom.

I'm scared
of these feral shapes.

These demons and
dark monsters

promise annihilation,
all they want is destruction,

to see their prison burn

and the gate of
their cage   is
rattling   now,

the   hinges   are   almost   loose,
a little more and the deed
will   be   done.

They come   to   smother
and   smite

with   avenging   fury
all   that   has   shattered   my   soul.

THE BLADE

The hidden depths
of night
come through
sharp breaths

each pang
or fizzing ache

needs to be
met and faced

the keen edge
of the razor's blade

must be felt
as it slides along
my skin
and draws blood.

Is it orgasm
or some other
relief

that comes when I meet
the drawn blade
and trace its wake
along my cut flesh?

How I want to turn away,

to believe this pain
was never here.

How it changes
when I face it,

so large
I might just break
or dissolve

into the dark pit
that's been closing in
all these years.

The tear,
   the tears,

they are here.

Do I have to go
into these dark pits
of nothingness?

As I ask the question,
I know I have no other choice.

DEVOURED

A corpse, still warm,
lies on the earth.
By it two are crouched
taken by the feast.

Only when they turn
can we see
two parents,
devouring their only son.

HIS BODY WAS A BRIDGE

His body was a bridge
between worlds,
the one we all know
with Tesco and Sainsburys

and the other -

the one beyond the veil
which exists
as a waking dream,
where an owl squawking
at daybreak
is a poem that touches
the very heart of fear.

And that fear
has place
and lives.

It wants to speak,
so it shows up in dreamtime.

It comes out
through beings met on wanders
that leave you confused
and amazed at the mystical possibility
contained in the world.

His body was a bridge
between worlds,

the scars and cancer
helped him cry
the grief and anger
he held all those years.

He feared to express
the raw truth of his soul,
he feared to show up
as himself.

But when he broke
open with screams
and agonising wails

he became something more.

Broken open,
he's a servant to all,

he gives his body
to the fall and death
of this once great civilisation.

MAGNUM OPUS

Can a diamond come from ash?
What if a myriad of forces
pushed and pulled,
squashed and squeezed
the flocculent mass
into something,
                              a shape,
it never knew itself to be?

What then?

What would come
from such work?

Maybe a diamond,
or something else?

Maybe the mass
is being worked
by something greater?

Maybe the precious stone
is being cooked on the
alchemist's stove?

But its folly to take
the cloudy stone

for the final work,
the completed opus.

How I need to stay in the fire
and allow the lips of flame
to march and patrol,
ensuring their destruction
is complete.

Making angels in the snow
of the form that once was.

Making angels in the snow,
laughing.

How will I know the work
is ever done?

Maybe I will only know

when death's rattle
rings in my ears
and escapes my throat -

maybe there's no knowing,
just letting the turbulent forces
continue their ravaging ways

and whichever way I choose to step,
whatever act I choose to live,

I pray not to spoil the work.

THE VORTEX

There's a vortex,
it seems to suck me in,
spin me around
and pull me down.

No matter
how hard I try -

    flap my arms
    or kick my legs,

        struggle for breath
        and pull myself out,

I cannot.

My limbs tire,
my muscles begin to ache,

    the tongues of surrender
    whisper their wicked spells,

        allowing sleep's weight
        to have its wicked way,

but something, Estella maybe,
comes forth at that time
refusing to be smited.

It seems to find me
in my muscles and bones,

    'Go on!' its voice urges,
    'Continue, carry on.'

        It knows
        there is still
        life for the living.

Its not yet time
to yield

and allow the indomitable
to swamp me over.

    'Carry on,'
    the voice echoes,

        so I listen
        and find some resolve,

although, what's next
I am unsure -

all I know
is I must fight.

RESURRECTION

Crumpled to a heap -

the exhausted remains
of who I was.

Let go,
I've let my shape

come crashing down
over and around me.

The relief and joy
of surrender,

letting go of
all that kept me strung

like a puppet or kite

filling out a shape
that was never mine.

The blessed heap
of tattered remains.

Pieces here and there,
limbs and flesh
of the one that was.

All that's left
is my voice.

The one constant
that can speak these words,

that observes
the chaos and carnage
of the one that was -

no more.

To stay in this crumpled place,
and hold myself
in this formless shape,

to be the puddle
unmoved in its crevice,

moving
only when moved,

responding
only when called,

staying in its place
with the agony of being still,

with the thrashing
sense that shows

there is one
who is passing
who still needs to die

and when he does
the heavens will descend
with their weight
and press onto the ashen remains

until a gentle breeze
will stir and breathe

the being into something
he always was.

The jolting awake
will come in an instant

and the shudder
    and choke
        and scream
            will sound

from virgin lungs
with their very first breath

singing,

"Resurrection."

THE WORK

This disease that wants
to kill me
is actually here
to serve me.

Its a perilous road
of healing
but the journey is yielding
many riches.

I'm being forced to move
and shift,
to face and see
all at the heart of it...

and I won't ever
have a doc
in a white coat
say,
       "Yes, that's it,
       the reason the disease came,
       these were the lessons
       for you to learn, so
       you might grow, serve
       and be all that you were
       born to be."

Instead the knowing comes
from those fleeting moments
that linger as frozen shapes.

Sometimes these forms
are indistinct
but they resonate
with a golden hum.

This being. This truth.
This gold
              just exists

and its only when
I lift the edge
that I catch the affirmation.

Its no coincidence
that the shit
comes up now,

at this time in my life,
in these moments

that make me cower
and shrink,

carrying the dull pangs
of long carried ashes,

my frame shakes
in a way that
unsettles the very root.

The tears are in my throat
and they cannot be soothed.

Its the things
I've lived - those people,
that place,

which help me see

        that, oh yes, actually,
        its been here all along,
        its been like that for years,

        I didn't think
        to catch it or name it.

The sphere of invisible bars
that crush me to a shape
that's never me.

I step out and away,
breathing relief that comes
from space

I feel the magnitude
of the tasks still before me -

to change and transform
the relationships that shaped me,

to challenge and confront
the toxic dynamics
that suppress my
true shape.

The ask is nothing short
of taking a stand

for myself,
for them,
for Life itself.

This, my friends,
is the work.

I AM HERE

I am here

       my goodness

I am here

       drawn out
       and dazed

I am here

       breaking the bonds
       that kept me small

I am here

       standing tall
       with pride
       and grace

I am here

       calling Mother
       to hold me

       telling cancer
       I am giving all I can

I am here

       wiped and spent
       from the effort

       of forging my soul
       in the crucible of Life

I see myself

       and hold him
       with adoration,

              'I love you
              dear friend

              I know
              you will go
       till the end.'

       Something's been shed
       a sapling grows,
       now a tree.

       Belief
       is here

       rooted
       and tall

       I stand

arms outstretched
to the endless night
inhaling Autumn's chill.

I howl
with all my might,

I am here!

THE WOUND

There's a lesson for me to learn
so deep and unsighted
I've not known that I've
needed to learn it.

It comes as the cloak of my wound,
the one that shapes and drives me,
the one infused into all that I do.

I've been unable to see it,
to recognise the pathology -

the smallness of my actions
rooted in a frenzied pursuit of survival,
of making my way in the man-made-world:

of having place amongst my family,
of being respected by my friends,
of being fulfilled and completed
with a hollow sense of self-worth.

I've not seen that my drive to make it,
to stand in the world as 'success',
has been the very ill at the heart
of my plight.

Only now do I see,
with death knocking at my door -

I've one last chance to face it,

to embrace it,
to know it,
and transform it;

to be an agent of life
by truly living from love,

to bear my gift to the world
through the chalice of my person

offering the sweet wine
as benediction,

my only intent to enrich
and know whats mine
and whats not,

to dispel the rot
and act from an integral wholeness,

to know that there is only one space
for love in the world

and that my life is given
to embodying and expressing
the shape of it.

Revelation

ALLOW IT

Allow it

to find you
to take you

and run itself through
your body

like the most sensuous
saxophone you
could ever imagine

or allow yourself to feel.

Let it in
let it take you

to places you've never known

just trust the player

coz the tune

is unlike anything else
you've ever tasted.

Its nectar.

Its the place
where words begin and end
serving as accents
to the melody playing out

right now.

Let it find you

and when you do
allow it to run through
and saturate
every fibre of your being.

THE WATERS OF SOUL

The prince soothed his finger,
pricked from the rusty cage,
from whence he'd released
the wild man.

Into the depths of silver
he dipped his sore finger
to see gold, on withdrawal,
where the wound once was.

The rivers of soul flow up from below,
places of darkness and gold.

The darkness scares us
with shades of decay and deformation.

The river flows
inviting us to go down to the depths
of despair and suffering.

Taken to limits of breath,
from the edge and beyond
what do you find
in the place of shadows and no form,

where time is unknown,

in which echoes of gifts
clamour from the walls

enclosing your truth -
that you built in the life that
was never yours?

The crushes and crumples
of forming knocks,

the imprint of your soul
is the same shape
as a star that shines
in the purple heavens.

To see with open eyes...

To be deaf to the singing stars
is to deny the glory,
of the song playing out

right now.

MAGICIAN

Three lines meet.
Each boundary contains

the sea,
the wind,
and land.

Only fire knows,

what is known by each
together and alone.

SEED OF STONE

A swallow soars through the wind,
its wings expanded and wide,
the elements surround it,
but all life is inside.

You are the seed of stone
that belongs in the face you broke from.
Now your journey is one of return
and leads you to places
you have never known.

You are called to be strong,
to be all that you are,
to be like the stone
and withstand the elemental forces
that have shaped you.

FINDING THE SHORE

The screw turns,
the fire long cold
still burns hot.

The memory of a dancing flame,
invited to spark from dream
up into voice and movement.

The voice breaks
from rememberance

unsure where the root lives
or how the memory begins.

Through her phantom form,
the nemesis speaks
of all that wants to live -

for she knows the power
that comes from liberation.

DARK STALKER

Have you felt the terror before?

It comes in the chest
born from the waves
building and growing
surging and passing
before...

    crashing - BOOM

It comes from the cliff's edge,
the wind shakes my bones,
its howls beat my legs,
splintering rain on my face.

The behemoths overhead
move with such speed
they dump their seed with indifference.

Its the night, at a time
I feel I might just die -
such relief to awaken
to the first grey rays,

but the terror
with each crashing wave
carves greater space within me.

From its place
I feel something moving,
lying in wait -

      a predator

with the power
of the wind, and the seas
and the mighty land
that birthed me

with the dark skies
and its stars shining brilliant,

it rises from their void,
it meets the crashing waves,
I pray the cliff will hold me.

I'm beginning to understand
that I have all of that power,
all of that Life within me.

Is it that,
maybe,
that scares me?

OLD MAN

How fiercely I've brandished the whip,
fervorously frothing at the mouth,
foamy spit and the crazed look in my eye.

Same as a crazy old fool, his head
a nest of unkempt knots, oppressed
by a stagnant cloak of piss.

He has holes in his shoes,
so I can see his toes. He even
has a dog in tow. He stops

every now and then. Not to
observe, or be still, or absorb
the glory of life, no.

He stops and yells, "Fuck!" or
"Shitty cockballs," or "Arrrrggh!"
shortly followed by incoherent cackles,

unaware he inspires avoidance
from those around him. Mothers with
young children cross the road. Young men

give him a wide berth.
A pack of friends spur each other
on, pointing and laughing, hiding
behind their false bravado.

This man drives me to insane lengths.
I reflect his frenzied demeanour. But I know
how to hold it down, or when I scream

and break, I know to do it
in the the depths of the trees, or
behind closed doors where no one can see.

And because I'm not mirrored,
because my insanity goes unseen
I can pass as normal...

But instead of keeping the old man away,
what would happen if I went up to meet him?
If I gave him my ears and dared ask

what he needed, and why he was here?
I'm sure for a while he would not know,
that he would be unable to comprehend

my acts of care - for so many, for so long
have derided and rejected, ridiculed and mocked.
He may be confused, or aggressive,

non-responsive, or incomprehensible,
but with time he would get it.
Something would get through. He'd understand

that somehow, for some reason I exist
and I care. And through my affection
he would thaw and face to meet me

and our eyes would meet for a moment
and I would come to see something so familiar
it would feel like a cold, sharp dagger

plunged into my pulsing heart.

I would see myself in that man,
looking back. I would see myself
and I would know the need to hold him close,

to give him all the tenderness
I was never able to give myself.
I would know the importance of being soft

and accepting. To invite him into the space of
my home and love him

and love him
like he was my very own.

SHARED HUMANITY

There are moments
in which I feel
I am not alone,

I see the colours
of a tie dye throw,
or the love made
in a picture,

sometimes I'm caught
by the image
that is cast in a poem

or by music played
and created from a place
no mind can fathom.

These portals of knowing,
they find me.

I see into them
as they reach into me.

For a moment,
all that overwhelms me
is soothed by the balm
of remembrance, that

I am not alone.

There are humans
that have been

there are humans
that will be

like me,
like so many of us
right now -

on a journey like no other,

to know what Life is,
to sense its meaning,
to know enough
to be free in this world.

OUR LOVE

To breathe is to know
what this between us means.

Home, first is anchored
in the cage of my ribs
infused into every fibre and sinew
of who I am.

Wherever I go
I take home with me.

But, you see,
alone I am still incomplete.

I only know what it means to live
when I remember your lips on mine,
when our fingers interlock
and our skin sweats together.

Lost in the depths of your eyes
I find myself in a home
of a different kind.

This one is larger.
This one seems boundless.

Its like - alone I am alive,
but with you - something more lives.

Our love is a being of its own kind,
our love is an essential act,
it brings this one to life -

more lives in this world between us.

Somehow it is greater
than anything I have ever known.

I feel myself thirsting for it
when we are apart
just needing to be sated
by the waters that it brings.

You see, I love you,
but I serve our love.

I wish to nourish it
and tend to
whatever need it may have.

This may mean I say no,
or I meet you at my edge.
It may mean I cower or explode
or shy away from the tasks
that need meeting.

But I know that you hold me,
that you cherish our love also,

that you call me to meet you
in a way that is sublime.

And you hold me in my shame
you do not judge or berate me,

you only call me to myself,
invite me to look at the places
I daren't or which I overlook.

This task of growing down,
and filling out

makes me
writhe and shake,

sometimes I successfully escape
from the tasks that need tending
so I can honour all that lives
between us.

And sometimes I spit bile
or the filth I've pushed down deep.
Sometimes I reject or play out
in waking sleep
the patterns of my own wounding

and I know these creases,
these folds and tears in my person
are the gaps through which
the life seeps through.

But I want to drink from
the hallowed cup of our love.
I want to be filled and nourished
and sated.

And I'm learning with time
how I need to put myself
on the line,

bare myself on the altar of life
and give myself over to the service
I say yes to.

You may complete me,
you may fulfil me,
but my path is my own to walk.
You cannot walk it for me.
You cannot save me.

All you can do,
the one ask I have

is that you love me,
that you hold me,

and when the house begins to shake
I ask you to take my
hands in yours,
hold my gaze and allow
all that we share
to move between us.

This is how I dare to love.
This is what I dare to give.

To this one adventure,
the life that we live,
I choose you as my companion,
my co-conspirateur -

lets dance beneath the
stars, through fields of golden
corn, laugh our way to
perfect laughter

and know, *just know*,

we are alive,
we are in love,
we give ourselves
to the good fight
and trust.

Aho

A QUESTION
A NOD TO UNCLE DAVID

Have you ever made
an unspeakable vow -
one that would kill you
if you broke it,
one that would break
if you spoke it?

ITS LATE ENOUGH

The journey of descent
   and return -

slipping through the net,
   camped beyond the veil
      to encounter

images that come as whispers
   and dance in a way
      my body remembers.

These images of dreams,
   seen through the earth,
      live in the realms between us.

To be with the dream
   and live it through my body
      so it forms
         the shape

of my being,
   my person,
      the way I live
         in the world.

To be with the dream
  so I know
    I am

        Earth   Flesh
        Water   Blood
        Air   Breath
        Fire   Spirit and Soul

my single task in life
  is to answer the call

rooted by the wilds within,
  I'm rising to embody
    the true shape of me.

Enough searching
  and questing,
    now is the time for enacting,

its already late enough.

Epilogue

THE POET

I am a poet, afterall
lying at the edge of the world,

with neighing wild ponies,
and rustling cautious mice,
the chirruping chaffinches
bring me to know life.

I am here with it all,
far from the filth and noise,

elated to be on this hillside,
in the throes
of an advancing Spring.

The daffodils are disappearing,
rowan leaves are emerging,
the air is imbued with the hope
its lightness brings.

I wouldn't want to be
anywhere else -

an observer of the great,
a reveller of the majesty.
And these heavy, angry voices
which preach hard work and industry

can do one.

Being here on this hillside
is the greatest expression
of living I can muster -

watching the world pass by,
knowing my place amongst it all.

I need to dwell here, at this edge,
on this lip and bare witness,
celebrating existence,

harking that this here,
basking in the sun,
drinking the rich,
refreshing breeze,
revelling in the birdsong
is an essential act.

Through this I know myself,
through this I know the world,
through this I live a little more.

There is more of me here.
There is more of me here.

Only when embodied
can I know I am blessed.

With these riches
my life is worth the battle

of making ends meet,
standing on my own two feet
as a True Adult in this world.

I am a servant of Life

dancing like the sacred fool
imbued with the funk that comes
from giving no fucks, invested in
the one thing that matters most.

You know of what I speak -
that one precious thing,

because when you feel it,
when you know it,

there can be no other way.

THE GIFT

It doesn't matter
about recognition
or validation,

that's not the point.

Nor is being able
to put a crust
on the table
through it,

although
it would be nice.

The important thing
is the enactment -

the embodied expression
of the one thing
you cannot live without.

And if you did
your life would be grey,

and if you did
your life would be flat.

Do the thing
that makes your life pop

that makes you fizz
and brings you to sense
what life really is.

Of course,
there's more to it
than that:

building a life
from the soil
of your values,

standing upright
and living
with integrity,

there's coming home
to an animate world

and there's also
coming home to yourself.

I see
I've been so caught up
in trying to 'make it',

needing to feel valued
and loved,

that I've overlooked
doing what I truly love

the one thing
only I can do
that no other can;

I may do it
in a cellar,
or out in a shed,

I might do it
pre-dawn,
or quietly in my room
post-sunset,

but I do it
with vigour and zest

and if I ever step from
the safety of my harbour
and share my gold
with other souls

then the world
and life
will be truly blessed,

because I am sharing
my one true gift
with all.

ACKNOWLEDGMENTS

Firstly, I would like to thank cancer for coming into my life and for reshaping me as it has. Many of the poems in this collection only came to be because of you.

Secondly, I would like to thank death. Your presence in my life has shaken me deeply. But you have also enriched and guided me. Thank you for inviting me to live the essential. To midwife this project that I needed to live.

R.H.

Robert Howe died of Cancer on October 27th 2023.
He completed this collection a week before.
This body of work is his in its entirety.

Robert wished for nothing more than for his writing to
inspire and nurture others on the journey of soul.
He also wished for his words to be a web,
weaving soul pilgrims together.

If you would like to share anything about your experience
of this collection,
or if you would simply like to connect,
please don't hesitate to reach out at:
soulpilgrimcommunity@gmail.com